# Amazing Americans: Susan B. Anthony

Stephanie Kuligowski, M.A.T.

# Consultants

**Shelley Scudder**
**Gifted Education Teacher**
Broward County Schools

**Caryn Williams, M.S.Ed.**
Madison County Schools
Huntsville, AL

**Publishing Credits**

Dona Herweck Rice, *Editor-in-Chief*
Lee Aucoin, *Creative Director*
Torrey Maloof, *Editor*
Diana Kenney, M.A.Ed., NBCT, *Associate Education Editor*
Marissa Rodriguez, *Designer*
Stephanie Reid, *Photo Editor*
*Rachelle Cracchiolo, M.S.Ed., Publisher*

**Image Credits:** Cover & pp. 1, 8, 18 Alamy; p. 5 History of Woman Suffrage/ Google Books; pp. 3, 10, 12, 19 The Granger Collection; pp. 18, 21 iStockphoto; p. 20 Avery Kuligowski; p. 21 Stephanie Kuligowski; p. 7 The Library of Congress [LOC Memory_rbpe 13700400]; p. 4 The Library of Congress [LC-USZ62-111870]; p. 6 The Library of Congress [LC-DIG-ppmsca-11398]; p. 9 The Library of Congress [LC-USZ62-46713]; p. 11 The Library of Congress [LC-USZ62-46701]; p. 13 The Library of Congress [mnwp 159001]; p. 14 The Library of Congress [LC-USZ62-95344]; p. 15 The Library of Congress; p. 16 The Library of Congress [LC-USZC4-5585]; p. 17 The Library of Congress [LC-USZ62-60762]; p. 24 The Library of Congress [LC-USZ62-95344]; All other images from Shutterstock.

**Teacher Created Materials**
5301 Oceanus Drive
Huntington Beach, CA 92649-1030
http://www.tcmpub.com

**ISBN 978-1-4333-6982-7**



Printed in Malaysia.
Thumbprints.45293

# Table of Contents


Family Beliefs . . . . . . . . . . . . . . . 4

Speaking Out. . . . . . . . . . . . . . . .10

Big Dreams . . . . . . . . . . . . . . . .12

Lifelong Activist. . . . . . . . . . . . .18

Amazing Americans Today. . . . 20

Glossary . . . . . . . . . . . . . . . . 22

Index. . . . . . . . . . . . . . . . . . . 23

Your Turn! . . . . . . . . . . . . . . . 24

# Family Beliefs

Susan B. Anthony was a smart and strong woman. She believed all people are **equal** (EE-kwuhl).

Susan was born on February 15, 1820. She grew up in the state of Massachusetts (mas-uh-CHOO-sits).

Susan was born in this house.

Susan B. Anthony

Susan's parents were members of a religious group called the Quakers (KWEY-kerz). Quakers believe all people are equal.

Susan's parents wanted **slavery** to end. They thought slaves should be free.

These slaves are planting sweet potatoes.

## Slavery

Slavery is when people are forced to work without pay. They have no **freedom**.

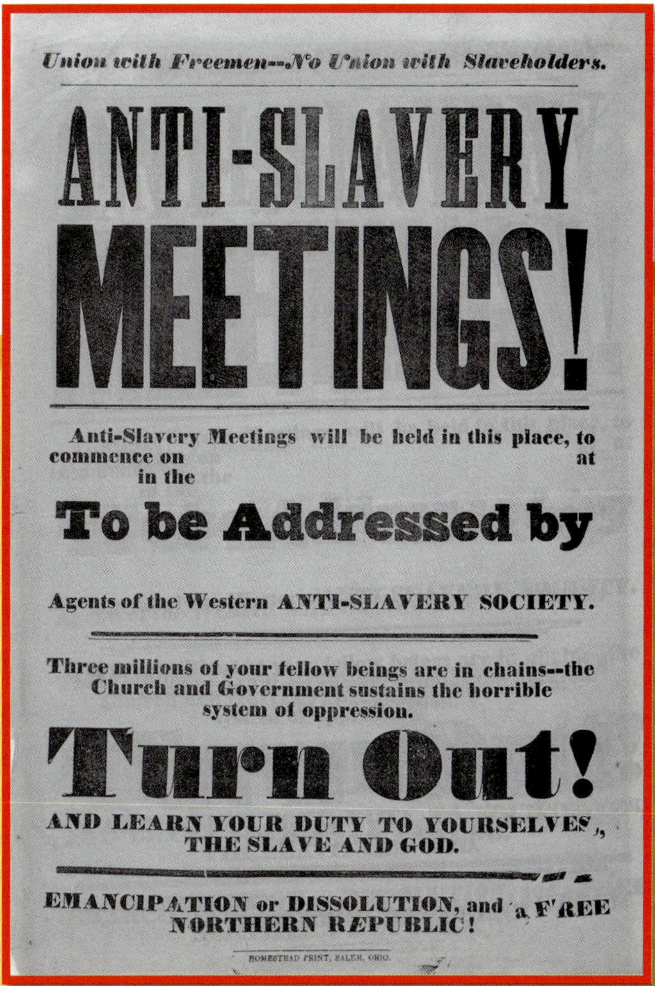


This poster tells about meetings to end slavery.

Susan was a bright child. She could read and write when she was three years old. Still, her teacher did not think girls should learn the same things as boys.

Her parents did not agree. So they taught Susan at home.

Susan reads as a grown-up.

## Favorite Books

Susan read many books. One book she read was *Jane Eyre* (air). You can still read *Jane Eyre* today.

*Jane Eyre*

# Speaking Out

Susan grew up. She became a teacher in New York in 1848. She earned $110 a year. Male teachers earned about $400 a year. Susan thought this was unfair. She wanted better pay for women.

This is Susan as a grown-up.

## Family First

Susan gave her parents her paychecks. She helped them pay their bills.

Susan lived in this house in New York.

# Big Dreams

Susan wanted to change the world. She believed all people are equal. She fought for the rights of women and African Americans. Susan wanted to change the way people were treated.

Susan tells people about equal rights.

## Best Friends

Susan's best friend was named Elizabeth Cady (KEY-dee) Stanton. Elizabeth also wanted women to have equal rights.

Susan and Elizabeth

Long ago, men had more rights than women had. Women could not own a house. They could not **vote**.

Many people wanted to change the way women were treated. They wanted women to have the right to vote. This right was called **suffrage**.

This postcard tells why women should be allowed to vote.

# Women's News

Susan and her friend Elizabeth started a newspaper. They wanted more people to read about their ideas.

The Revolution.

*PRINCIPLE, NOT POLICY: JUSTICE, NOT FAVORS.—MEN, THEIR RIGHTS AND NOTHING MORE: WOMEN, THEIR RIGHTS AND NOTHING LESS.*

VOL. I.—NO. 16. NEW YORK, THURSDAY, APRIL 23, 1868. $2 A YEAR. SINGLE COPY 10 CENTS.

The Revolution.

ELIZABETH CADY STANTON, PARKER PILLSBURY, } Editors.
SUSAN B. ANTHONY, Proprietor.

OFFICE 37 PARK ROW (ROOM 17).

*THEODORE DREAMING, WITH FLAG AT HALF MAST.*

Last week's *Independent*, in a long column, throws Mr. Chase overboard, clears the track for Grant, and gets itself ready to wheel into line with the multitude in the coming contest. After the most unequivocal praise of "the Chief Justice," the "President of the Senate," "Salmon P. Chase," after making a profound bow to him in each of these capacities, admitting "that his life-long convictions have been in favor of liberty, justice and equality; that he holds to the civil and political rights of all American citizens, without distinction of color [illegible] advocacy of Mr. Chase for President now ends,

stitute another name, it might be the name of Charles Sumner, or Schuyler Colfax, or Ben Wade, or Gen. Butler. But, of course, the Chicago Convention will go pell mell for Gen. Grant. Nevertheless, we shall go on dreaming our day-dream of the happy day when only a great statesman shall be eligible to preside over the Great Republic.

This happy day is to be ushered in by teaching the people how to choose their leaders; that the best interests of the nation do not depend on the success of any party, but on the virtue and education of the people. Why go "pell-mell" for Grant when all admit that he is unfit for the position? It is not too late, if true men and women will do their duty, to make an honest man like Ben Wade President. Let us save the nation. As to the Republican party, the sooner that is scattered to the four winds of Heaven the better. If those who speak every week to 75,000 subscribers "dream" when they should be wide awake and at work, "a Great Republic to preside over" will soon be a dream also.

E. C. S.

*ANNA WIDE AWAKE WITH BANNERS FLYING.*

more easily led *en masse* than the more cultivated Mrs. Howards.

People who see two right sides to a question generally fail to see either side clearly. All questions of importance, such as relate to human rights, are so perfectly clear to those who see them at all, that both the right and the wrong side stand out in bold relief. It seems to us that neither Gail Hamilton nor her reviewer comprehends the deep significance of this question of universal suffrage. In reading this book we were struck with its weakness the moment the author lost sight of Todd and undertook to reason. Like the cat with a mouse, she was wide awake and intensely active until her victim was no more; then came a reaction that left her foggy and dull through many intervening pages, until at the close she awoke from her nap and ascended into the higher realm of prophesy and speculation. After boldly asserting woman's right to suffrage, we were surprised at the flippant way in which she disposed of woman's duty and dignity in the exercise of their political rights. After annihilating the Rev. Todd and clearing the battle-ground of all [illegible] instead of rebuilding on the spot some marble

This is Elizabeth and Susan's newspaper.

People worked hard for suffrage. Susan and her friends marched in parades. They gave speeches. They also had meetings. They did not give up. They wanted women to have equal rights.

These women are marching for the right to vote.

## Behind Bars

In 1872, Susan voted. This was against the law. So, Susan was **arrested**.

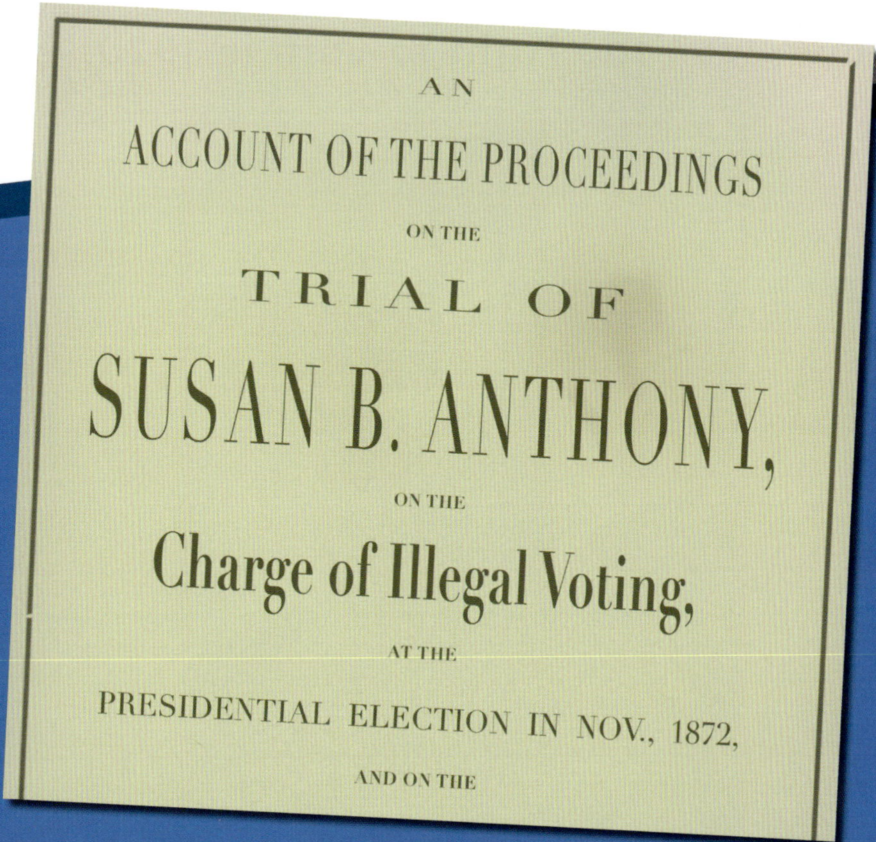

AN

ACCOUNT OF THE PROCEEDINGS

ON THE

TRIAL OF

SUSAN B. ANTHONY,

ON THE

Charge of Illegal Voting,

AT THE

PRESIDENTIAL ELECTION IN NOV., 1872,

AND ON THE

Susan's arrest was a big news story at the time.

# Lifelong Activist

Susan was an **activist** (AK-tuh-vist). She took action to make her world a better place.

Susan saw the end of slavery, but she never got to vote legally. She died in 1906. Women won the right to vote in 1920.

This woman votes in 1920.

## An Honor

In 1979, the Susan B. Anthony dollar coin was made to **honor** Susan.

This coin and stamp honor Susan.

# Amazing Americans Today

Susan B. Anthony was an amazing American. She thought all people should be equal.

Today, there are many amazing Americans. They work hard to help people, too.

This drawing shows Meredith and Madeleine helping people vote.

## Ask It!

Ask an adult to help you find an amazing American in your town. Interview the person. Find out what he or she does to make your town a better place.

Avery is a first-grader in Illinois. She interviewed Meredith and Madeleine. They help people vote in Crystal Lake, Illinois.

# Glossary

**activist**—a person who takes action to change things

**arrested**—to be taken by the police to a police station or jail and kept there

**equal**—the same

**freedom**—the power to do what you want to do

**honor**—to show respect for a person or thing

**slavery**—being owned by another person and forced to work without pay

**suffrage**—the right to vote

**vote**—to make an official choice for or against someone or something

# Index

activist, 18

*Jane Eyre*, 9

Massachusetts, 4

New York, 10–11

Quakers, 6

slavery, 6–7, 18

Stanton, Elizabeth Cady, 13, 15

suffrage, 14, 16

vote, 14, 16–18, 21, 24

# Your Turn!

## Your Rights

This postcard tells why women should get to vote. Think about the way people should be treated. Make a postcard that tells why people should be treated fairly.